Know LovƐ

By Judith J. Willis

Formatting and Editing by

Judith J. Willis

Photograph by Rosemary Lamon

Cover by Chanice Gray

Self- Published in Canada by Judith J. Willis

ISBN 978-19990228-5-3

$14.00 CAN

TITLES BY JUDITH J. WILLIS

Illusions

Curse Of The Time Witch

Words Without End

I'm Still Here

The Patterson's Men

Verses in Poetry

Sweet Pea

KNOW LOVƐ

DOUBT GIVING CHANCE

This is the face; my heart yearn to be near

This is the face that cause me restless rest

This is the face

This face, that could do me no wrong

The face that make me walk around blind

Oh! On high clouds

The face, my beacon

The face that erase all obstacle within my path

Oh my ever rest

I have live ageless time to feel your cheek upon my face

I have wondered seas to grasp a scent of your fragrance

I have live a thousand lifetime to cast a glimpse upon a fraction of you

A face that cause me restless rest

Shadows of memory past

Be still my beating heart, that break of a sudden sound

Of a disappearing spear

Like shattered glass, figments

Spectre, phantom far from sleep, my eternal rest

NEVER BEFORE

I've never been in love before

When you look at me with your baby blue eyes

I feel butterflies and shyly smile

My tongue is falling all over my feet

Is this how I'm made to feel?

Awkwardly, excited and frighten

The wind take me to new height, the world stop around me

My enchanted flower

World apart, this could never be

Stop before my heart beats

For I never been in love before

Carefree, the whispering of the breeze carrying secrets

Shhhh!

I must confess to my Priest

I run away in flight, this is how my feet travel

I've never been in love before

I could never open that door

NEVER DOUBT

When the coins is low, have faith not doubts
While in wakes in the paths of no doubts
Have faith and not doubts
For the Lord is here, have no doubt
Fear not, for he has not forgotten you!
In your doubts when the times is low
Fear nor doubt can't hide the bridge to the paths
where he wait to lend shoulder of no doubts
Come sit with me and have no fears nor doubts
For the paths ahead is clear, have no fears
For I hear you my child
For I see the shadows simmering in doubts
Awhile longer. Have no fears nor doubts
For all your prayers will be answers
For in your fears and doubts
The paths is not straight, hardship lingers
Narrow and straight
For in the glory is the light before your eyes
Fear not! For I hear your doubts and I will sit with,
you in shadows and doubts
When your fears is not doubts
With my arms outstretch to console you
Come take my hand and walk with me on this bridge
into the moonlight

MADNESS

I want to wake up in this madness, that is your arms
The way your kisses tingle the skin
I want to be drown in this sea that is your eyes
When you hold me tight, in your arms the world is
suddenly, alright
I want to go crazy with you, the person that you hide
behind your eyes, because you let loose with me
tonight
Thank you for giving reasons to appreciate this
magnificence sunset rising
For in this madness, it's alright because your mine
I want to get lost, in your eyes, escaping this for
awhile on the back of the motorcycle ride
The wind is whipping me into smiles
Later your mine
I want to get lost, in this madness, because you are in
my life
I never want to wake up from this beautiful madness
that you are mine
Life is precious, it could be lonely but never when I
look into your eyes
I'm spellbound by your madness that you brought
forth into my life
When my skin tingles, only you seem to do
Say you will be my guy, until I draw my last breath
I wanna stay in this madness and I hope you feel the
same way too
I Want to get lost, in your forever

UNWANTED

I don't need you riding my shadows
I don't need you calling me up late at night
Crying your tears
Tears of I don't know how
Saying that you are sorry
You melt me and tear my world apart
You can't change the past
I can see the road, clear as I look at you now
I 'm writing my own verses and show you how
how I'm going to live
Break down these walls brick by brick and show you that
I mattered
You try to break me a child, once love
My head can't process this mind games
Throw my number in the trash, like the bruises across my
back, I will climb these ladders way up to the sky
Don't call me up late at night
Saying you're sorry
Behind your lies, I see you smiles
I'm here to stay, take your sorry and get out of my life
When I see you coming, I don't know if my foot will hit the
brake
Walk with me, when you were my reasons to smile wearing
matching clothes like you tattoo your soul onto my heart
Take a ride with me to the wild side
Come sit with me, reminiscing the moment when we first
kiss, a touch of sparks flying

KITE FLYING

I stumble in my drunken state, hazy in my wakes to
be consumed in loneliness, consumed in what
I thought is the moonlight
I find myself here to a path of nowhere
My head in the toilet in puke and nowhere
And not realizing how my feet brought me here, to
this place in this place of nowhere
To face the bleak reality, climbing off clouds
From my high on booze and God what, nowhere!
Climbing of the clouds in my hazy state,
Trying to find or recall my car I have reach the
streets of nowhere. Finding faces, no recall of names
Finding faces of nowhere
In my gloom I presumed, this is life flying on high.
The in-crowd, to make mother proud
To see my face, the gutter rat
Flying high as a kite
The big mighty and proud

LOVE

What in a name to call my love, the fair!
What in a name when my heart call to you, my dear!
What in a name when I see you everywhere!
Awake or asleep I see you clear
Yearn to be near, my love. My dear
Reminiscing the tingles of skin
The touch in sin,
Yellow rose the color of my love
Watching the flow of oil
Laying on my back watching the ripples of the tides
What in a name to call my love, to see and touch your hair,
the feathers touch of lips to be lost in nowhere!
My love, my love
To love you, my soul call you here, the sound of your
laughter
Time, time, my love I wish you here!
Back to the past to make you appeared
To sing a song, a song of how love brought you here
The name of my love who never appear
A name, a name, a name of my love
To make my heart sing and tingles of the skin
What in a name when my heart calls you here!
Paradise is not far when I looked into your eyes
It's here in your arms
The name of my love......
I speak your name... Jason to float and soar in heavenly
sky
What in a name, my love, my love

RIPTIDE

I die the day you refuse to look into my eyes
One magical night you held me tight I wasn't your bride
It's eating me up inside
I take a motorcycle ride
It's weighting me down like a stone to the ground
Riptide as the current shifted
Riptide to love a man in sin
The stone I carry around, is weighting me down, down to
the ground
Never sorry, I didn't know how life could be so
complicated
On the bench watching for the evening tides
Waiting for the sun to rise
Waiting for the feel of the morning dews light
Riptide the current tides
On the shore
Watching the moonlight rise

RISK

My domain, look to the right the caution signs

Trust is a two headed sword

The road more travelled is doubts

Speak to me of flaws, speak to me of hidden walls

Welcoming you into the arms of our lord

In the circle escaping the darkness I see into

your soul, the hunger, the desires

My comrade, touching your skin is the holy grail

Demon speak to me, in your disguises

Drinking from lips, oh what bliss

Your mirage of what never exist

Welcoming you into our circles, open your self to

me

Bade in the glow of our Lord for he is king

Be the witness, the chances, the risks

Faith is all

Come!

BACKWARD

I love you like you love me.

I wake up in the morning

Smile across the love that is my eyes

I pray the lord for this beauty who could love

and break me

I want to walk on the wild side with you, back to

the times where we were young wild and free

Back to where love see no reason to judge

Back to where my eyes see you as my guide

Back to reasons, only when I look into your eyes

Back to reasons only you and I

I love you like my heart do

Even when I'm feeling blue

I love you I just do

The better part of valour is discretion, in the which better part I have save my life.

Falstaff
Henry 1v part 1
William Shakespeare

BARE

You strip me bare with a single stare

Quiver and stares

The stars alight, the stars align

To live in faith hands

To meet in the place where heart beats

Faith, destiny don't leave it all to chances

Make your own leaps of faith

It this, where you 're meant to be?

Here on this planet with me

Wisdom can be deep

Answer this! Where are you meant to be?

My heart leaps at the sight of you

Take the leap and lets faith do what she is meant to do

Waiting for the man in dark blue

Waiting to the moon to set the mood

Waiting.......

AT LAST

At last I have escape the bullets in the streets

I have escape your smiles and big feet

At last I can soar

At last, at last

I'm proud to say I'm not trapped by your belts and welts

I'm free to be me, at last

I'm sorry to see you go, with a hint of doubts

My lung, I release thee, air to breathe

I run wild, naked in the streets

So, look at me running wild and free

Oh Jehovah! Look at me!

Releasing the lung, I'm free, I'm free

At last to be me

World look out! For the sky is my limits

The beast, the beast is dead

Trumpets and horns loud blasts

Running wild in the streets and jumping trees

At last, at last I'm free!

The beast, the beast, the beast is dead

PASSION

Passion in our hearts as you gazed

Passion is what drives us, mold us, shapes us

Passion lit the fire that burned deep within us

Passion is passion

Passion is raw and pure

Passion is what hold us

When I look at you, I witness the flame

When you speaks, I see the fire burning

This is when love speaks

This is my passion here with you

My heart is you

Passion, this be you?

ILLUSION

Vexed in my realisation that I'm in amore
Time stood still and I has not manage to pull myself off the marry-go-around
I see you in mirrors and I can feel your breath against my ears, and I enjoyed the throaty sound of your laughter. I hide behind closed doors, cowering.
Too old to mend my ways, too afraid to hold hands
Vexed in my heart, it will not lead to a new path
Afraid to even glance at the picture of you, afraid to feel that pain once more. I come to the realization that in my heart and soul. I have love you near and far and in my heartache, the thoughts of you lingers
A touch of glass
A glance at the moonlight we once shared
I can no longer lay where we once shared; I wake up haunted and afraid by the traps of memories doors.
The figments of my illusions clawing to be free. To speak your name, tingling of the skin set cheeks to radiant light
The image of my illusions to mirror a mirage
To love and hold dear, my illusion faulter
To light fire, to walk ablaze
Stroking cheeks with the movement of hand
So soft the radiant light to look at you with midnight
You're the threat that binds me

KNOW LOVE

When a boy kisses a girl
It say I like you
When a boy holds your hand, it say I think of you
When you're on my mind, I think of you as my bride
Know that you are loved
When a boy kisses a girl, there are possibilities
Know that you are love
When a boy calls just to say goodnight
Know that you're caught
Know that you are love
When a boy looks into your eyes
Know that this is the moment or never
Know that you're loved
When a boy brings you flowers
Know that he's guilty
Know that your thoughts are set asunder
Know forgiveness
This is the turning point
Know what is in your heart
Know love
Do you think this is worth the fight?
Know that you're loved always
Know love

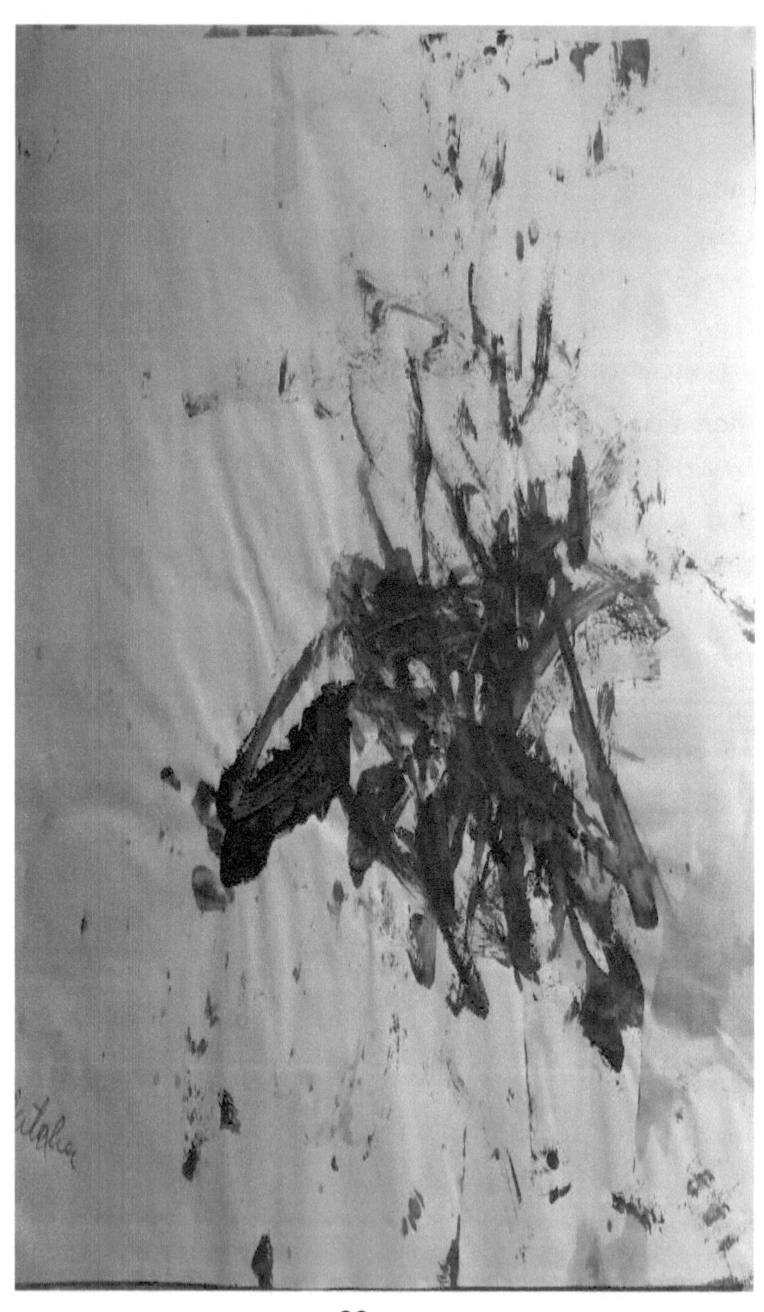

THIS BE LOVE?

What In a name when thy love is untrue?

What in a name when thy love knows your name?

What! Be this love?

Held in arms and know love

When mothers hold you, could this be love?

When at 3 am eyes wide awake imagine starlight

Could this be love?

Feel shivers, feel tingles of skin

Recognizing your scent

Know when you are near

This be love!

When eyes are closed, the catches of breath

Could this be love, this be love?

Love, love. What is it to be in love?

Do I feel love? Do I know love? Do I recognize love?

In confusion that is thy mind.

I'm in love? This be love!

AH! IMAGINE!

Ah! To drink from what I imagine is to be your lips

Ah! The taste lingers

I closed my eyes and thought in wonders, what it feel like

to be held!

Apollo, my God I call to thee in radiance light

I command thee, brings forth to me

My love, I wish to see

In ancient time I pray to thee

For thy Lord, thy God is jealous as should be!

The lamp that burns, to shadow thee

I pray to the Lord thy God that brought me to be

I beg of thee in my old age

Lets me glance of the face of my love to be

For this time, I haven't met thee

I pray, grant me of a single glance

Of my love

To rest in sleep eternity

DEAD END

Dripping from my blade
I can taste the blood
Like a beacon beckoning me home
Look what you've done!
Razor sharp, slinging like a gun
I feel the blade slipping from my grips
You have to face the priest
In the pile of blood down on one knee
Hail, hailing for Mary, mother maybe
Slicing from limb to limb
Good God man! What have you done?
You are losing grips of reality
What this cause of insanity?
Listening for the call
Brother, you gotta get a grip!
In the shadows of doubts
This is not some dark fantasy
I hear the sound of the Angel wings
Coming down to console me
She said, boy look at me!
I find myself in sleep of harmony
Yeah, as I walk in the valley of shadows of
darkness
Thy rod comfort me
And so, it begin

LOVE GODS

I speak of love; this city girl seek nor believe in love

For it pained me, to witness this overuse word in love verses

The hourglass of the sand of time, to say who live or dies

The Goddess of love, Cupid arrow? What will they think of next?

I call to thee; Cupid where is the arrow that is meant for me?

Is love real? Show me for I have not seen nor hear how love comes to be!

Be it Venus or Cupid

How love came to be?

Wild and free melodramatic free

Take me on your wings

Apollo witness come before me!

SILENCE

Silence is a deadly thing

Too much time to ponder about various feeling

Too much time to remises

Time, time is a deadly thing

Give me time and I will tell you why

Too much time to get the gossip right

Silence to rot inside,

I look inside minds in the blackness that is behind

the eyes

Fall into nothingness, falling endlessly

Complete silence, oh so deadly to be silence

To imagine the unthinkable

Silence the calming rage that fill me

Silencing

Slicing into the moonlight to the depth of
nothingness

Shadows is where, you hide in the sun on the back porch

In my sunglasses I watch you shimmered

Shadow in the air

Dark bloomy cloud, phantom be gone from here!

Judith J. Willis

IDENTITY

The curvy winding road as I watch the waves heaves
As the rushes of water tickle my toes, to be a child again
laughing and giggling. The sway of the waves as it mold the
sand so. The rushing of the waves pounding upon flesh
Young and carefree as I let my hair down. The sky
suddenly open to cleanse such as life
As I feel the coldness that compel me as the sky pour
down on me, I sense a change in me, I couldn't grasp what
it could be, my heart suddenly beats
My feet compel me to move my feet, eyes on me beyond
the trees, my heart compel me to beats
My heart beats faster as my feet dragged me
And there lay why my heartbeats
It suddenly dawns on me life how it could be
My heart control me, to taste your kisses
The winding roads I couldn't see
Lover reaching out to hold me
Life flashes before me, it dawned on me why my heart is
not complete
Lay before me on the concrete, who I would to be
As the sky fall down on me, to kiss your feet
Wings freed me to be on my journey
Crashing waves beneath feet
Tears on my cheeks, as I turn from the heap
This was meant for me if I was on time like as always me
The winding roads and the paths that lead me to the heap,
suddenly it dawns on me, beauty, and the beast

DO I KNOW LOVE?

To love, to love I don't know, what the fuck
What do I know about love?
Does any of us really know, truly know about love?
Know love!
It's our hearts or our mind tell us that we are in
love? Know love!
When we see that someone, that special someone
That our heart recognizes our heart rate escalates
and palms clammy
You feel scared and excited at the same times.
Is this love? Know love
When you are kissed, you are caught into
nothingness and you swear you hear cheers and this
unimaginable excitement
You are not scared, you are just in a state of
blankness, nothingness
When released from that kiss you are smile and you
feel like dancing. Is this love? And suddenly once
again you can hear everyone else and for a tiny
moment you wonder where did you escape to? Know
love! And look into each other's souls and overcomes
with shyness
Is this love?
Know love!

REACTIONS

Chemical reactions, the lingering of skins

To sin is to kiss your skin

I gladly sin

To be lost in the depth of nowhere

The blazing bed burning

To witness the touching of skins

Roaring the sound, the thunders roaring or is my heart exploring

Glide, slide comes to me into the moonlight

Flowing, spells spellbound binding me

Chemical reactions exploded when skins reacted

Substances equilibrium

FIVE DOLLAR BILLS

On your platform with five-dollar bills hanging out of
my panties, high on booze
Working to live up to your fantasy
Trying to burn out misery in a bottle of tequila's
My disguises is the evil smiles
To keep your hand where they're meant to be
I wake up and look into your beautiful eyes
I shrink away grab all my clothes and run out the
door, escaping with my life. Why I'm still here? Why,
You, laugh at me sir! It's not funny. Volume speak to
me
Think about life swinging from trees to trees.
Imagine how carefree that will be!
In life six to midnight, I put on my disguise
Spinning tales of lies
Shaking my booty for silly smiles of five dollars a
song
High on booze, as I watch the sunrises in your eyes
Swinging from trees to gained five dollar tips
Oh! World what have we become? Silly and carefree

BUTTERFLY

Like a butterfly emerging from its cocoon

Life is in bloom

Watching it delicate wings flapping away

Life is in bloom

Beautiful and sweet, beauty is she

Life is in bloom

Watching as her wings flutter away

Life is in bloom

Before your eye's mystery in disguises

Life in bloom

EYES, PARADISE

Here in paradise on the edge of the world
I can boldly say as I looked into your eyes
Would you hold me last night?
I fight in struggles and triumphs?
In your arms you hold me tight
I can see doubts, as you try fighting to answer right
Shall I kiss you goodbye?
Your struggles in doubts
Or do you need a moment to think
Baby it's alright
There is no right or wrong answer
You are the fire every torch needs to light
Right now, I'm burning bright
To witness the sparkles in your eyes
There is your answer as I look deep into your eyes
There is hope, have no doubts
I'm here as long as you wish it
Oh, to be true, to be kind
You're the engine that I need to start my heart
Please don't abuse it or I will crumble to oblivion
I'm here to mold you tight if the need is deep
It's alright, please baby don't cry

THESE ARMS

These arms, they don't hold you the way I do

For you once said, they're your security blanket

Now they just don't hold you right

I never know someone to complaint so much

About security that use to hold and squeeze tight

Do tell, the reason why?

These arms can do you no harm!

These arms is to mold you, to touch you,

to be kiss by water and suds,

these arms that doesn't feel right,

they cut you up like knifes,

these arms no longer console you,

these arms

Why, Collatine, is woe the cure for woe?
Do wounds help wounds, or grief help grievous deeds?
Is it revenge to give thyself a blow
For his foul act by whom thy fair wife bleed?
Such childish humour from weak minds proceeds:
Thy wretched wife mistook the matter so,
To slay herself, that should have slain her foe.

The Rape of Lucrece
William Shapespeare

TOO LONG.....

For too long I hide in shadows.
For too long, for too long I spend many hours not sleeping. I kept it all hidden inside for when you peel away the layer, I know you will not accept me. Beauty is not skin deep! For I'm not ashamed to say this is my foundation that molds and shapes me, to stand tall. For I have accepted the me that I'm proud to be. For the roads is rocky, this battered broken down me who has witnessed far too much, for too soon.
For something so simple as a hug, should feel so strange to me. I 'm no longer feeling trapped and incomplete. For I recognize the face that belongs to me. I can see eyes, nose, cheeks without dimples. With my spectacle I witness eyes that shine brighter than the starry sky.
I greet you with kisses, for this is me who I'm meant to be! What it's your answer to be? The brand new me, beautiful me, the bitch that I could be. Unique me, for the world can deal with only one of me, that I have discovered living in the old me. Again, I'm asking not begging or pleading, just so to be clear on this topic.
Will you accept me?
I'm still me. Again, will you accept me?

YOU

You're the picture I look at when I'm feeling confused

Frozen in silence, could this be you?

I'm losing time

You came to life

To ever think this boy is mine

Stay awhile!

Until the evening tides to witness the docking of

ships, as tide waves in

Maybe I'll find the man of my dreams

Wouldn't you walk with me?

Until the sun leaves the sky

Till morning light

Tell me how to improve

To make you see if I'm the moon

The glass moon rises, to see into souls

The leaf turned into snow

As my glass moon rises

COURAGE

Fearless, resilient
I'm me
I have come to this
I don't have to explain myself
I got here fighting despite the hurdles, the obstacles
I'm here
Be brave, own up to your truths
The bitch that I can be
Allow me to clear the path of being, the human, the animal
There is no in-between this is part me
The fighter, the cherry pie
Part me, part beast, unique me
To have the courage my love to be brave, to be me
Part saint, part evil
This is me, not on my knees
There is no breach, this is truly me
I'm still here
Existing because of you, you're invisible to the eyes
For you couldn't see this is me
Flaws and all, human being

MILES

I remember the hurt, as I refuse to look into your soul

I watched the door for miles

I listen for the rings of the phones

Hoping you change your mind

Something so beautiful could never be mine

The crashing of the waves as I'm about to lose my mind

Life, oh life to hurt for miles

The clouds and sky goes on for miles

For miles, for miles I run and hide but you were here at my side

Why life choose you as part of my life

The pain of chaos inside

Life goes on for miles

I refuse to accept that you are not mine

I understand why the pain will not leave my side

This is life without you here at my side

The upside sun, the crooked rains fall

I wish for this pain to subscribe

INVENTIONS

Scattered amongst the grains of sand

My lovely love

Scattered amongst the chaos the doubts

My lovely love

Scattered amongst the pile of ashes the love that

survived the earthquake

Scattered is the love that could outlived the stars

Scattered my heart, my hourglass

My lovely love

Scattered, crumbled

This!

This, is how man falls

Outreach, out class the hours glass

The glass moon rises

This fail inventions

MOMENTS

A moment to shine, moment to make the world mine

A moment to turned head,

in moments to know that you're mine

A moment to make the sunshine

A moment

In this moment, I can see the possibilities

A moment is all I needed to make you mine

A moment

A moment

A moment and forever you're mine

in moments

SMILES

Your smiles is the reason why I'm caught up in these disguises

Words fail me, as the wind captured your scent

I know you are within distant

Smiles

In your smiles I witness your hesitation

In your eyes I witness your crime

It's your charm, the shyness within your smiles

Don't witness claws

Inspired by the radiance, your smiles

NOWHERE

I sit here in this place that I now come to recognize

The soft stillness

The calm quietness

The hours when I die

The so soft stillness of the heart slowing

Weeping in frozen stillness of silence

Arms reaching to what

The clutters of straws

The slowing of heart

Goodbye my ever-beating heart

And lips tremble into smiles

FORGOTTEN

Forgotten, you where once the sky

Forgotten breath

Forgotten movement

So stillness the shadows embrace the dark

You belong to me

Come slowly, come surly

Come to me NOW!

The years has wither away waiting for the

movement that was once heartbeats

The stillness in the grave, as life call to me once

again

But, soft! What light through yonder
Window breaks? It is the east, and Juliet is the sun.
Romeo and Juliet
William Shakespeare

THE EVENT

The event

Movement of death calling names

Everglade as the butterfly descend from a life well

spent to answer the call,

The siren songs to bloom and blossom

To pluck from bloom time consumed

To woo and swoon to play games time spent planning

In suspense to go about life in events

Roll call, so simple the mind

Feeble fine

SHIELD

I'm no one, I'm everyone

I ventured where smoke screen appeared

Strayed into the cold

Ventured where hearts bend

Into the heart darkest of men

I'm what you desired; what hearts craved

Power to speed up went sent

I'm what lead reach out what sent

I'm what the heart truly craved to have absent

I'm what you can't erased darkest of men

I'm as should be, the bravest of men

The ever last, the conquered, never the dark

present

Nice
JAMAICA
Luck
Of the
Irish

JudetH

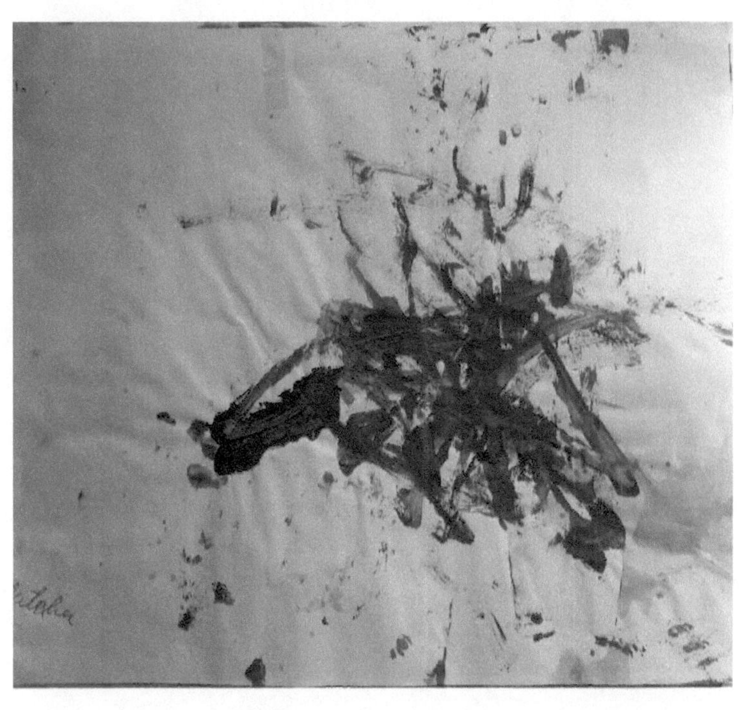

SKIN SINKING

Scale every inch of skin

Waves sinking in

It is a crime to enjoy such simply dance

This be bliss?

Name your price I gladly pay the price and do time,

for my crime

Waves crashing in

Your cuts and dices

All the magic in life couldn't pieces back the tears

in the dice

All the tears couldn't fix the stars swirling in

space

Sinking, sinking

SWING THE MIGHTY BLADES

Trust is two-headed swords that can cuts and dice

Swing left, swing right

Meet evil, route 66, where the sun meets and kisses the sky

Ticking to wasted times

Scale the balance

Is ten years enough to seal the deal?

To sing and dance

Beats evil with goodness for all the cockroaches and

mice will come out when the price is right

Swing left, swing right

The sharpest of the blade is the swinging of the

tongues, gossips open doors to chaos

Swings of the blades turn to guns

Trust, the two-headed sword swinging where bullets

The strongest of tongues

The mightiest of blades is the sharpest of tongues

UNDERNEATH

Here I stand, in this world or beneath your feet! I can say my loving you is free. Free as the heavens above. Free to wonder the world above or below, but you my angel know no boundaries. Always finding new ways how to hurt me and call it love. Love that feels no pride, love that's only to cry, you want, want, want only to want never to give. To give me up, holding me down only to bound me. Bound me to the ground where I can no longer feel or see the heaven. Say you love me only to wound me., Say you need me only to bleed me. Bound me to the ground where commanding is to make me understand my dignity, stronger than we, braver we be. Understanding your need to only make me beg and bleed to see the need and your greed. Strip me down to ground naked and proud. Where I bleed rape and in this belief where you claimed. You want and needed me, where you make me go hungry and in this belief. Where you cheated to make me understand, I did not fulfill your needs. In this belief I cried and wanted to die. That loving you only hurt me. You take all my pride and joy and bring me to the bad man land, where griefs and unkind is all I can understand. You make me understand someone of my kind doesn't or should not have the attention of a kind mind. To go mad is all you understand, to treat me unkind! Making and wanting me to understand who above mankind. Strip me down, spit in my eyes to make me want someone of your kind. Prove to me that wanting and needing you, is never a kind mind. Wanting and needing is never my place. To bow down on my knees is the right place to be. Dawn to dust, my weary brows. Only to feel, to teach that loving you is never letting me go. Bound me to the ground where the heaven can no longer breathe. Loving this man this man of unkind. Evil in disguises.

THE ANIMALS

Creeping crawling, the animals comes to play

Crawling on walls driving me insane

Crawling upside down the wall

My mind can't tolerate the insects tiny little feet

Prancing about without cares or defeats

The animals, part me

Creeping and crawling which is not me

Going about freely, hearts see no reasons to bleed

Tortured and tormenting of me

How you invade my home, like you are footing the bills

The animal how they take possession of me creeping on walls

Silence of the hills

The animals

STAIRWELL

I'm not always there, look to the sky rainbows and other wise

Look to the sky and see all the reasons why

Look to the reasons for,

why you and I alone exist

I sit in the stairwell drumming thoughts

Thoughts of when I see the unwellness in smiles

CONSUMED

Consumed in the limelight

Consumed in greed

Consumed

What is expected of me

Consumed

Consumed

What is real

Consumed what is make believed

Consumed in this made real Hollywood fantasy

Consumed to witness this tragedy

Life or make believe!

Consumed! Consumed!

Consumed to live out this life of how you view me

Unique human being

VOICES

The sounding of your voice makes me weep

Whispering, calling to me

On knees love to be, come to me

In times of need bowed down only to me

Perfecting of a voice that now belongs to me

The swirling of your Latin tongue

The only word that is recognize to me is amore

Feeble faith to love to define

The joy of words as define in one true mind

Amore' te amo

For a hawk, a horse, or a husband?

Much Ado about Nothing

William Shakespeare

HISTORY

Parched world

Looking for quenched thirst

Carrying on with centuries of graces

Parched to journey

Near and far

Parched for knowledges of disasters

Parched on the strolls of time

Parched for centuries

Century pasts

Parched to look into the hourglass

BLACKNESS

The blackness in me is willing to fight, willing to be set free. The blackness in me can't make you escape, or refuse to acknowledge the beauty that is me.
Free to express, my God given right
I know you don't want to see me
To treated me as the invisible shield
To erase me, the individual
Think what you will, learned from an open mind!
Think what you will learn, aaahh! the blackness
Think with free wills
Freedom of speech, think freedom
You have no reasons to chain and cage me
The keys you so proudly dangled
You have no power over me, so I believed!
When my eyes are closed your knife and guns
Are loaded to the dime. You hide behind idiocy, mockery. Face me! Be big and proud!
For bearing teeth's, can't hid smiles
For the blackness is real

SECRETS

Whispering as the wind carrying secrets

Sheltering on display or dismay

Travelling the world and back to the sunny day

of May on whence the wind came

The over play of the wind dismay

Wavy waves trying to reach the caves

Rushes and clashes of the wind

In the afternoon in May

MY BABY

My baby is gone! Gone with winds of dawn
I can still feel the warmth of our body swing like straws
My baby is gone
I don't know where or why but he is gone
After loving in first light like a soft clay that find purposes
My baby is gone
Gone without kisses, gone without explanations
gone without care
My baby vanished!
Do I care?
On my neck I felt tremors, gone without causes
Baby vanished!
On wings of times I didn't master the disguises
Faults are blamed
My baby simple vanished
untoward

SURPRISE

Surprise that your smile looks into my eyes

Surprise that you want to hold my hand

Surprise that you see the beauty

I so proudly hide

Surprise that you want to give time

to spend absent life

Surprise as you hold me

It brought tears to my eyes

A touch of care

A human touch

Lost in exile

TRAPPED

Screeching and scratching creatures wanted out

Wanted to be set free

Trapped in the everglade

Screeching, loud screeches

Trapped in this god forsaken place

I don't know where is here

Trapped into this madness that is my mind

Trapped forever

Seeking to be set free

Lunatic is set

LIFE

I have aged watching the world in chaos

Hoping they will learn

And witness the damage

Parasite, Lunatic, when will they learn?

In time it will vanish, disappear

Freedom will be a thing of memories past

I will disappeared and still they will not learn

The lesson of human kind

Compassion, accepting what and those we can't

change or hid the body

The madness, the genius

The simply of things of life

SHADOW FALL

I have walked in shadow

I have walked in rain

I have walked in snow

Where ever feet may go

Back to nowhere

I have walk blister and all

Shadows take me to falls

Be lost and be found

I have dragged my feet across the board walk

I have mellowed out in the park

Bear witness of the fall

They are willing to watch and laugh

When will this fool learn

There is no place for you in this world or beyond the plains

Be gone beguiling fool away from fears

To be, or not to be- that is the question.

Hamlet

William Shakespeare

PENNIES

A penny for thoughts, a penny for naught

Which ever men lay

He paid not in penny but more dollars in coins

Be weary, old man farts

Scream in mirrors, see tiny feet

Which ever way you bend

Whispered, don't tell a soul

The talk of towns

The bitch, for a few gold coins

I can ride the horses noon to midnight

A penny for naught, a penny for thoughts

I am at sale price to satiated with no return stamps

Dry like prune, feeling rotted and blue

Witness bruises

For I'm labelled and priced

I'm at your command til the music stops

Noon til midnight

A penny for thoughts, a dime for a song

When the music stops

PLEASE….

Take your gloves and hat

No kisses on lips, I wish not for my heart to

the fantasy realms

I wish

Oh well, a girl can choose to wish

For it's a fool game not to realize my place

On four was the score

Never on my back

Who want to look in the fucker eyes

I have mirrors to see if the need arises

Before you greet me

Sir… please leave your coins by the door

Standing or kneeling, come time are a wasting

For the clock struck the hours

There will be no midnight hollering

TOUCHING

A whisper, a touch this lonely girl sees through your disguises

For smiles dinner on dimes

Croak on lies, witness wedding bands

See the tired lines

I'm your fool, your monkey in the streets

Lonely and blue bear witness

Loneliness is better than being blue

Tired of lies, for reasons you hide

I'm neither to make bride or makes nice

Fucked for whiles behind evils smiles

Night, night, say hi to your wife

Branded at an earlier age

Laying on my back listening to lies

I had no choices, battered, bruises and cries

Follow the map and find a dime for pennies

For I'm not royal, I will wash your behind and eat wheat flop

I'm not your princess, the soft touch as the tides wash away

midnight to November or back to once where we laid

ONE MONTH

It lasted a month beauty and bliss you hold me so

easily marked and felt trusted

To be fool again to set up with arms

To think this girl, ever deserved a dime or a happy life

Accept that you're marked for life

No happy life. No man wife, unwanted child remained

undiscovered, untapped

You were never meant to shed light, be gone monkey face

I vanquish thee

From whence you came, make head way

Obliterated,

Be gone you were never meant to breathe

Hands over thy face

Be gone, I vanquish thee

Blessed be

THE CALLER

On my knees I bleed, the blood run deep
The scratches on knees
The preacher, how you have condemned me!
I watched as the shielded statue laminated proud
Blood dripping from skulls
What does it all mean, when they try to run, the
oppress, the greedy
How the mighty fall
Race through time to climb the mighty wall
Threaten, cornered

FAINTED SPEAR

I open myself to you, such mockery to be unwanted
seed, why mother abandon me, why father disown me,
why families shy away from
The mark of the beast, no loving arms surrounding me
No one to shape and mold me
Naked in the street, nobody notices me while I run
wild and free
Invisible to witness blood bleeding
With no one standing there, just a faint whisper of a
spear
Lamppost be my guide, mockery in disguises
Only dogs visit me once in awhile
The echo of teardrops to water the crops
No one care or hear the faint sound I make when I drop
Faded within the grass
Silencing the fall of the spear as it whispered and
disappear

PAST LOVE

How you creeps and crawls avoiding even the scent

from my thrall

I was once your maid

Made to entertain, now I'm a fallen leaf

The wind captured me and witness bruises

How I walk in limps

When even a kiss is a fist

Blistered

Pleading with the wind is a thing of past, love and

hate blistering in my ears

My fallen leaf crinkles

To loved or truly hate

MY DOVE

Perched on a limb waiting for night to approach

My dove

Waiting for you

Perched on a limb waiting to fall

The time, the distance of the call

Patiently waiting to fall

I'm still waiting

Faith, should I make the call?

Drowning in despair to repair what was once in the air

Mirage!

THE MATING DANCE

Searching my lips. Words failed. In kisses I forget how to breathe, moments to forget life misery and hails. Two lover souls in glow of love match in fights and chaos in the dens of lost and forgotten, we ride the waves of midnight mass as my husband claim me once again as his bride. His kisses make me weak in the knees, thank heaven I'm beneath him for surly I would I have fallen on my feet in the blackness of the abyss. He claim me as man and beast. As we swoon higher and higher to catch our breath within reach of the stars. The liquid feels of our body I'm forever in thrall as the rides of the pulses, as my husband moves above me, I hang on to his shoulder for dear life for no words can truly describe what I feel inside. Oh! we rides the winds of time, the winds of chaos, the winds of hope and freedom we ride as I lay beneath him, we ride for all the missing moments and chances encountered we ride as our life depends on it. The only sound in the room is the sound of our ragged beating hearts. As we swirled in the liquid of time my heart is aglow with lights of midnight that truly this man is my love match. As he kiss my shoulder blade and travel to my breast, the music master make my body sing in oohs and awes as the final pitch as the intro simmered and slow we collapse in heap twined in the bed sheets. How can he find energy to kiss my brows after this rises and falls of the mating dance. Sleep overcame me and I fall softly into the black abyss of blackness of the mind

Floating languidly reaching to the sound of the dance to mate

FEEL

I feel so alone living with a man that doesn't want

to know me, to get the balls rolling

Under the skins to be sun kiss

Where did I go wrong, after you hold and kiss me

I find my corner and cry, this loving fees wrong

I 'm sad and lonely

When the key tuned in the door

I fix my face

This is no fantasy or games

Why do I feel trapped and confused

It's so easy to end life in time and dues

When you look at me? Do you see the girl with her

arms open wide?

Damn, this ain't life

BECOMING

Becoming, how you mock and make fun of me

In breaches or panties, this how you see me

The grain of sands of a girl becoming a woman who

once believe in rainbow and fantasy

The only real games grown-up plays

Becoming a girl, scorching the sky

Leave room for flaws

I uses to think princess and fairy-tale are my life

dream

Luckily, I was slapped out of this fantasy

How you gaze languidly at me

As I bloom and blossom in becoming a woman

NEW

A new day, a new dawn, a new candle alight

To witness what God has planned

A new dawn alight

Cry and triumphs

Look to midnight

If you prick us, do we not bleed?

If you tickle us, do we not laugh?

If you poison us, do we not die?

And if you wrong us, shall we not revenge?

The Merchant of Venice

William Shakespeare

BEAUTY

Beauty the eyes don't see

Beauty, beauty beneath the leaf

Beauty the master of fantasy

Beauty manipulation and wasted teardrops

Master within the lies

Take the bloody bag for a ride

This bitch will never shed another teardrop

Beauty the stillness of the waterfall

WALTZ

Waltz, to waltz floating dancing in slopes

Crashing in heap of piles

Waltz floating in slopes

Wait while when it all erupts,

The cursing of the volcano, the rushing of tides

as I look to the sky

Waltz to wall

Waltz on the walk

WE PRAY

Standing silently

Watching

As monkey swinging from trees to trees

Idiots

On stages trying to impress me

Wakes in the everglades,

as we silently pray

THE BONE WEARY

Oh! he has come, the weary bone has traveled many miles, to bring news of plights
The weary, the weary bones to put meals on the tables
The weary plights, To make ends meet
We are Canadian, must work from noon to night
To pay tax, to eat and breathe tax's
Watch as prices of food run to the sky
The cost of living, put me to the street in card board boxes
The government allowed us to wear strings on our backs
While he eats fancy ducks, drinks champagnes
While the slums lords of the cracks
Makes us bleed and breaks our backs
Trying to live inside with freezing winter with straps on our backs
With no heat and holes dripping leaks smelling like shit or the dumpsters in the back
For we, the homeless, it's what happen when you closed your eyes to smoke crack, now weed is back so is the twitches, for I can think and breathe weed for everyone is smacked
Vape, vape for it about money, no matter how my heart swells and bleed, sixty the toll fall victims of greed laid dead for the price is not too high as we watch you stuffed your wallet

Come open doors to my palace, for the champagne has grown warm
For it's about the rich man seed
We must bleed only when someone die or ends up a handicap for us to mattered to makes changes
To hear my voices above the hurricane. To sued you for this is the only way to have life, to live and breathe air, for the law makes it easy to steal and cheat for this is how life is!
I can walk out the liquor stores stealing for the hard works that my heart pours
For the law in Canada says it is ok for you to steal from me five days a week before you are caught or have a busted knees
For the law is unjust!
Prove me wrong!
When I caught you stealing,
my calls for help is unanswered
If I calls you at one, I'm lucky if you come before the crack of dawn
Respect is what gets you there
For in my fancy jets, I looked down on you and laugh another day yet, or some more
For the teardrop in my eyes is running in over drives
For the silencing of my voice as I watch the crying world

What will it take for you to realize you can't take it
with you to the other life beneath the world or in the
sky
So lend a hand and listen to the sound of my voice and
see how I disguise the weariness in my voice because
it not easy to look you straight in the face and say
help just so that I can close my eyes to wake, do it all
again for this girl is not a rich man's wife
I'm weary, to stand up straight but, pride oh heavenly
pride will make me stand straight and will slough in my
corners
For we Canadian must work and beg with our signs for
the Prime Minister will not listen to silent our cry for
the moment
I don't have money for lawyers to fight you to look,
you straight in the eyes and say you have failed us
You have failed us Canadian!
As we watch the pride of our land
As they remove the red and white flag
Blowing in the wind in the northern sky
We must bow our heads and pray for salvation
For we, the white and red
Stand proudly for God, man, and country we Canadian
the white and red

ROXANNA,

My dearest heart I have live and die to feel the
warm of your cheeks, against my face
I breathe, you breathe, I move, you move
You are my light that cast all shadows aside
Your warmth throughout the night
Is my ever-burning flame
You are the reason, my life suddenly have purposes
Without you by my side, life has lost all its appeals
You are the fire; I wish never to diminish
Come to me in dreams
Come witness, my bride the beauty in my life as you
appeared before me
My heart beats for the first time when I saw you,
all the years suddenly slip away and life before you,
now is faded memories, I cannot think of a moment
when you were not in my thoughts
You are my breath; you are the blood flowing in my
vain
You have become the center of me
I will love you and only you till the end of me.

Garrett

CLOCK WATCHING

Watching the clock as the hours tick away

Life wasted as the train is late,

all will change in blinks of the eyes,

to minutes in may

and it takes a toll

Life on display, watching the clock tick away,

on your stage the monkey in cages

Trying, watch or wanting to escape

The flights on your stage

Clocks ticking away, midnight faze

38B

Witness come forth, has anyone seen or heard from the woman in room 38b,

She could be dead under a rock, is she not your neighbour?

Your friends?

Has anyone seen this woman?

Come crowd, come forth speak to me, speak up!

Anyone?

Our remedies oft in ourselves do lie,
Which we ascribe to heaven: the fated sky
Gives us free scope, only doth backward pull
Our slow designs when we ourselves are dull.
What power is it which mounts my love so high,
That makes me see, and cannot feed mine eyes?
The mightiest space in fortune nature brings
To join like likes and kiss like native things.
Impossible be strange attempts to those
That weigh their pains in sense and do suppose
What hath been cannot be: who ever strove
To show her merit, that did miss her love?
The king's disease- my project may deceive me,
But my intents are fix'd and will not leave me.

All's Well that Ends Well

William Shakespeare

MELTED MOLD

It's not being poor or black that you will not take me back
It's because I shined above the world and the sky
How you try to break my back
Try to trip me
Ripe me
And break my spirit
Try to turn me into a idiot with two left feet
Try to make me comply to have no life
With the belt across my back with the bruises dry and cracked
Weeks without snacks, weak and smell to break what you bore, simply as life to take knife and drawn back life
The mold you try to mold to perfect what you believed is flawed

CRACKED

As I look at my reflection in the mirror I smiled the
crease tighten
Not realizing this how they see me the aged, the
worn and the afraid, the spots that tell the tales of
life spend
The curve in my back that will not go straight
Who is this the mirror see, unafraid
As I looked the mirror cracked
For years you held grace and just like time the,
mirror cracked
For even the stillness goes weary after time
As I look at myself the cracked mirror

ONCE

I love you once, my esteem twice even a thousand time
Like the grains sand laid buried undisturbed
Love unadoring
Love scorching the sky
For awhile I feel the tickles of the sand
Unadoring the trickles of time
Once, only once, oh I feel the dawn light
The trickles of the stars
For once in dreams of dawn light
The feathers of touch
The softness of pillow flowing
For once come to me, blinded by the after glow of delight
Oh, softest of delight
Flowing so softly
Creeping to the tingles of rapture for once the sweetest soft delight
Chilling thoughts of the mind for once come to me where dreams doesn't exist come oh sweetest delight

THOUGHTS

I thought this is meant to be

I Thought this is how I feel

Scared and unafraid

For I no longer feel the cold

Your arms melt me so

Your eyes shut the door to those lay ashore

I thought nothing could open a lock door

For even I can't predict the hours of the time that lay before

For all the gifts will not allow you to open your heart

To run hands along cheek

I'm not what you seek, I'm what you uses till something better appear to melt your waiting heart

And there respect will make an appearance

For I understand where hearts truly lay

CODED

Crack the code the chilling of the soul lets the
secret be told once the secret is told the world
would know

The code of existent, the code of the world unknown

For more than a thousand years I stood before you,
in a world of chaos, in a world of hate

A world of wars and drugs

A world that will not disappear after I disappear,
and you're dead

A world of infinity

When your wars is done when you finish killing us for
a loaf of bread

I will still stand before you, waiting for lesson
learned

Coded world for there is no mystery to be solved

Your world is free to explore

Discover the mystery of life

Mine is here as I realize the safe heaven the
mystery of life

EASILY BROKEN

The heart breaks so easily

So easily broken a thousand time to mend

Hearts of lead heart of my stone

Resend what can't bend

Easily broken, the crooked sun

I see what you did when the deed is done

Hearts tied up in chaos

Hearts on a limb, heart disown me

Heart easily broken

DREAMS

All my haunted dreams is here in the daylight

I thought I have escape you!

Reality is calling to you, there is no escaping you

My heart on the ground, my direction is chaos,

haunting dreams befall you

Nightmare becomes reality

How will I escape you?

Before I pull the gun to my head in peaceful

harmony

GUN SWAYING

I know I'm swaying

I know I'm playing with a gun at my waist

I'm drawing, I'm a big man now

The gun is weighing me down

Why I'm swaying

Intimidating, swaying

Keep walking brothers

I'm waving

The gun swaying

I gut the man open with my knife

I'm guarding

Now I'm praying

FIRE

Light my fire
Capture my every fashions and desires
Light my fire, captured the white desire, it's fire
Light my fire, I want to stomp on your heart desire
Light my fire, this heart makes to scream desire
Make my skin tingle and crawl
Light my fire as night falls
I put on red heels to thirst quenched desire
The moist wetness of fire
Put out my fire tall dark stranger, name what in a name matter
Fire, fire truly is all I desire
Creep and crawl on four or against the wall
Fire, fire burned up desire
My red lips scream, release of desire
Burn up fire, fire, fire
Weak, weak my legs went asleep
My heart pumping heat, hand me a glass of water pause on thirst
Desire
Wetness run still desire
Fire, fire
Call the fire brigade to put out fire

WHITE LIE, BRIGHT LIES

Consumed in your lies, consumed in your tales to make believed fantasy

I presumed this is how you view me

Tall tales as I look into my jug of ale

Confused, confused in a word of confusions

Why you choose to betray me?

Why, you run your parade around me?

Running your mouth off can't control me

I walk with my head held high; my smiles touches the eyes. I will greet you pleasantly for the compassion in me refuse to bow to knees to reach you

For all the seasons you refuse to greet me swimming in your lies and make believed

For each morning I greet the world with dancing feet, bitch wanna break me for my laughter makes you questions the girl you're after

For reasons you think I don't belong in this world or thereafter, your lies is like dressing up pies you are evil, disguise, the devil must be your bride

VALENTINE

Valentine day is like other days

To put your hearts on display

Put in your place

The crinkles of the day

The beauty of hay

Valentine day's a hallmark holiday

Love, love over use word of love

For every day, the show in may

To wall in shadow or a Mary-go-around

Speak your truth, where is cupid arrow

that wasn't meant to bleed

FROM HERE

I can't be your everything's

Even your wildest fantasy

Dressed up in black lace panties

You said your piece

Darling, I ain't it

Not even close to the shopping list

All the missing years

Misreading what was in the air

MEDIEVAL KING

Brought before kings
Kneel for he is king
For crime I witness in your eyes
In the name of the king
Kneel for he is king,
your monkey in the grass
Jumping up and down like idiots
Looking through the hourglass
Wishing for time well past,
In my armor, my sword, your castle
My liege
Medieval king

SINKING

Sinking ships like tides moves slowly as time

I got caught into smiles

I know, you are standing by

Web of time

Like bridges under waterfall

Slowly such as time

Ship will never rise

Slowly as hearts die

Web, unspoken promises, it so juvenile

Frozen hearts lie

Feeling doesn't surface inside

Slowly sinking ships subscribe

Such foolish times

Good queen, my liege, I come.
And I beseech you, hear me, who profess
Myself your loyal servant, your physician,
Your most obedient counsellor, yet that dare
Less appear so in comforting your evils,
Than such as most seem yours: I say, I come
From your good queen.

The Winter's Tale
William Shakespeare

FATED PATHS

Fated to walk the roads in shadows

Fate, as I look at the sky and be denied

The curse that has befallen me

To walk without purposes, to walk the lonely road

That has no ending

Fated within the hourglass

As rain falls, my eyes is moist with dew

fated as no arms surrounding me

The cold enfold me

I accepted you with open arms

I recognize the disease that is within me

Chaos guarding me, guiding me to paths where no

reality exists

Fated, not to glimpse at the precious sun

A CHILD

Never will I feel the soft embrace of your cheek
against mine within the moonlight
I dream of you in my arms
That all I'm allowed, is to dreams in my life of make
believe. Shrouded in darkness that is night, a ray of
light what is like to have arms enfold me? Without
consequences
To run my hand with brush strokes through your soft
butterfly curls. To inhale the powder scent of your
innocent never missing the sound of my voice. To feel
your tremors in my womb, so scare without my life,
So cruel a life without purposes. The ever-grieving
loss of a love once shared. Hope against hope, be still
the beating heart. Will I feel love so freely given?
Without attachment the infested dream
Will I be whole again? Without purposes, without
hope. Fear live on!
Never will I witness blossom and bloom
I dream you last night! Without hope, daunting
Precious. You are the light to put out the flame
To make cheeks aglow
Precious, a love that never was. To kneel I
Bowed. Cold within tomb
legacy
Will I never look upon eyes that alike my own?

DRAINED

Drained of thoughts that was left behind

Drained of wither and aged grapes

Drained of what was once brain

Drained of feathers of dens

Drained trying to capture, what wasn't there

Drained of a life spent in grey

Drained as the bills pilled to the sky

The showered of snow has mellow out

Drained as I must look at life in details

Drained, drained, why must life look at me with only evils

Worked from early morn to break of dawn

To fill belly with crackers and crumbs

FIGHTING

I will never stop fighting

When they look at me, what do they see?

I will crawl out of the hole

To fight the fears that is my own

To fight for freedom to let my voice rise above what

is my own so,

that I can face you who,

try to run me down to the ground

Out of fear to see me rise above

Face my fear in the mirror

To walk the lonely road in shadows and doubt

I will crawl on four because my fight has began there

MY CALL

If you give me a chance, I would love until the sun
come down my song the siren song
Sure as the heaven open up
Calling my soul to play in heaven's gate, tell me my wait
is over as the sunset roll in!
I can hear the call of the songs of the sirens calling
me home. I wanna make this sunset last forever until
I'm old and grey until I can't feel the pain no more
Sitting on the veranda in my age old day. I wanna hear
you say you have answered the call, my siren songs and
my wait is over
Merging two soul as one
Say you will give me the chance to prove the world
wrong. Who has doom our love to the underworld, the
whispering of my name has make the wait worth while,
my love, my love welcome home to arms that will never
let you go
For all the sorrow and pain has made the wait worth
while and I'm finally not standing in vain
Just give me a chance to hold you close for my
rainbows I have found my pot of gold
Give me a chance to hold you close cause you're finally
home
My songs of the siren has finally answered, and you
are home holding me close

ALONE AGAIN

I wake up alone again as my eyes wondered around,
the four corners of the room that is now my prison

If You will ever come home to the warmth of the
love that makes you run away

The echo of silence as you refuse to voice

The wondering of hurts wrong,

as the snow fall and melt, away another day has
gone, and my hope is gently slipping away

To set my mind at ease in this cruel world of grey
I have love this man,

My love is not enough to make him stay

The hourglass as time slips away and all dreams
lost in make believe

All the empty promises has withered and die just
like your kisses and no goodbyes

EMPTY

The chilling in the bone has lead me to the window
To watch the brilliance of the sun
The oddest, of what can't be defined
Empty, cold of the chilling dawn
Can't explain the missing link in what has emptied
The mind
Cold calculated
Psychopath

CRUSHING YOU

One look and I'm crushing on you

I honk my horn to get you to pull over on the curve,

your music is up high

I'm losing my mind to make you mine

Bumper to bumper your speed is high

Pull over on the side, I want to get close to you

On

The inside

FALLING SNOW

As I watch the soft flurry fall of snow

the chilling after glow, morbid

Seasons ever changing from rain to freezing snow,

my heart chilled

To watch the white curtain of snow falling,

in dawn of morning

I dragged my feet to the window to witness

The witness of snow making ok

The curtain of innocent of the fall of snow

As I witness my heart coldly display

CLOWN

I wanna marry you, clown face

I want a wedding in the month of June or May

Who would want a clown with a permeant happy

face?

The mask you wear to hide shame living on dimes

shedding lies

The straight jacket

The joker on display

The joker dined

Marry my clown in the month

of May or June

WAITED LOVE

Never rush slow beating of hearts as the butterfly wings flutter in dance

Caterpillar's in bloom into a elegant and gentle moth

Slowing hearts beats, the stroke of hands gently, brushes against cheeks like love it can't be rush, it can't be forced

Can't be denied

Slowly beating hearts, lovers kiss for the first time, the rush of waterfall

A thousand years you waited and then as if magic, washes all the sorrow with a single kiss disappear, a kiss lost in the everglade in the luscious soft sway

Of a lover moans

Of need

Stay awhile ......longer

GLANCES

When I was young I thought the world to be big
bold and scary
Feeling lost and unadorned
I wondered the sea shores
Trying to find shadows of a lost girl
So much noises in this big bad world that has turned
a deaf ears to wails of sirens and the echoing of
bullets
Swallowing, no mention of oxygen
The moving walls
The blanket over my eyes
Flashes of instants
of why I'm never found
The endless splashes of waves
and the stars to take me away back to once more of
Lollypop, rainbows, and kisses of the falling snow
The disappearing moon as the curtain closing to lay
ashore once more

ESCAPE

I wanng go, go away

Go to a place where it always snow where leaves fall

Because I shudder at snow

I want to hide away where my heart will not break
so fragile as the wind in may

I want my crawly space

Where the sound of shattered glass welcoming me
home to my deaf ears

I want to go away where I don't witness tears

The blanket over my eyes and still I can't escape
for feeling deep inside like a black tunnel echoing
reminding me that hearts still beats, after so
denied

In the wasteland, merry land, movieland there is no
escapes for you can run a mile, jump high

Life you can't hide, the thundering beat of hearts
waiting for ending to silence chaos for the mirror
capture what I refused to acknowledge that I'm
alive this is life

EYES

Into your eyes I witness stormy clouds

I want to erase the smell of your skin on the pillow

I want to forget the sound of your laughter

Like poison when taken to sleep for

A thousand sword piercing

I hate to admit you did make me smile

I want to forget the crumble crumbs along the walkway

I want to twirl around and never to stop

The touch of your lips

Denied the existence

Where is my magic wand?

MISTAKE

It could've been the girl next door

It could've be the falling leaves

So many reason why you smiles at me

A simple mistake but I was in your way

There is no substitute

For falling leaves

The nexus brought you to me

There is no substitute

This is our time to meet

In Fall watching falling leaves

You're my miracle, I didn't expect you

Now you're trails in the fog mist of memories

I hold my breath and to imagine the taste of your last kiss

I hear the thundering sound, the clash of my heart breaking, the shadow of you back in the fog

DAYS

Another day has come and gone, and I sit at my computer
Years has passed, my heart stoned
I listen to the sound of the wind as it carried the blasting sound of the neighbour's reggae music
Funny, how life take you back to moments, you wish you could freeze the time.
A simple silent whisper of a disappearing Moth
There must be a God in the heaven if above!
To make me wonder back to the lion's den
A million sunrises found you still absent at my side, silly things girls do,
Wondering if I imagine the man I once knew,
my heart beats faster of the thoughts of you
I smiled, feeling a little blue
Funny how unaware certain actions makes me think of you
Funny as time and years go by as falling petals and wondering thoughts of you
Days slipped into years

TODAY ALONE

For every doorway there is a window

For every window is opportunities

Open eyes to new possibilities

A simple hello

Open gateway

Every kiss is an adventure

Today is today alone

Enjoy the splendour of an elope kiss

Today alone enlightenment

Eternal mist, possibilities

Enthrall charm

Pondering upon lost causes

Today alone I marvel at the eternal sky

Such greeting

As I welcome new possibilities

With face point to the heaven

Look for three exciting new titles

Coming soon

Dating in the Electric Age

Flow

and

Alienelfskin

www.ingramcontent.com/pod-product-compliance
Lightning Source LLC
Chambersburg PA
CBHW021328060726
47591CB00006B/1915

* 9 7 8 1 9 9 9 0 2 2 8 5 3 *